THE SCREWING

OF

MR. & MRS. JOE

AMERICA

by

Michael Lameyer

authorHOUSE™

1663 LIBERTY DRIVE, SUITE 200
BLOOMINGTON, INDIANA 47403
(800) 839-8640
WWW.AUTHORHOUSE.COM

First published by AuthorHouse 03/10/05

ISBN: 1-4208-1190-8 (sc)

Library of Congress Control Number: 2004099363

Printed in the United States of America
Bloomington, Indiana

This book is printed on acid-free paper.

ACKNOWLEDGMENTS

This book was very important to write not only for my taking action but to help those that would like to take action but just don't know where to start. Much time and energy went into this work. My wife, Karen, and our children, Michael, Katherine, Michelle, and Colene always provided encouragement. I am also indebted to Quida J. Littles for keeping it real. Then there is Joe Kennedy, a friend who can be counted on all the time. My sister Patricia has always wished me well. Thanks to my mother, Sarah; who always taught me it was always too early to quit. Thanks also to Carol Ann Wilson, Russ Stiffler and Harry Thomas; better friends no one could ever find.

Thank you, the reader.

TABLE OF CONTENTS

CHAPTER ONE

ILLEGAL ALIENS

Fasten your safety belt and get ready for this ride, and if you're not mad now, you will be. First what is the definition of illegal alien? Broken down, you find the definition of illegal is against the law. Definition of alien is foreigner. Well then, illegal alien must mean illegal foreigner. Let's take a close look at what names have been and are being used to mislead you and me concerning illegal aliens. Some examples to be on the look out for: migrant, transient migrant, undocumented worker, foreign national, and citizen. That's right; can you believe it? The word citizen was used by President Bush. (Last week, Mr. Bush spoke out in favor of the immigrants: "Remember, we've got hardworking citizens who are willing to walk 400 miles of desert in blistering heat to find work," he said. [BBC August 10, 2001].) On November 17, 2001, "Senate Majority Leader Tom Daschle and House Minority Leader Richard Gephardt said Saturday that they would forge ahead with immigration reform early next year, including some kind of legal residency for Mexican migrants already living in the United States. Gephardt said that those who would benefit are 'people who have been in the United States for a long time, paid taxes, obeyed the laws, and been very good citizens.'" Oh Tom, and you there

Richard; you're talking about illegal aliens. Get it straight. Burglars are not uninvited houseguests. Bank robbers are not making unauthorized withdrawals. Illegal aliens are not undocumented immigrants and they most certainly are not citizens.

Jobs. It is estimated that illegal aliens displace roughly 730,000 American workers every year, at a cost of $4.28 billion a year, and the supply of cheap labor they provide depresses the wages and working conditions of the working poor, according to the Federation for American Immigration Reform. Despite being ineligible, illegal aliens get welfare the same way they get jobs: false identity and document fraud. In many cities, false documents can be bought on the street for as little as forty dollars. With false identity as a U.S. citizen, an illegal alien may establish eligibility for welfare. With the cost of displacing American workers, the cost of giving welfare to needy illegal aliens, and the cost of providing them general services, it is estimated that the annual net cost of illegal immigrants is $20 billion dollars (after counting their tax contributions). Remember, this only applies to the illegal that will even bother with the false documents. Many Americans need those ten-, twelve-, fourteen-dollar-an-hour jobs that illegals now have. You also need to know that many of the jobs held by illegals pay much more than some low wage, as we are supposed to believe.

"Business and social transaction costs rise as time, effort, and money are spent overcoming language and cultural barriers. Poor English skills among foreign-born residents cost more than $75 billion a year in lost productivity, wages, tax revenue, and unemployment compensation," says Ohio University economist Lowell Gallaway. Do you get it now? Do you really get it?

Medical Care to Illegal Aliens. You are not going to like this at all. "Mexican ambulance drivers are driving their hospital patients, who can't pay for medical care in Mexico, to facilities in the United States. They know that the federal Emergency Medical Act mandates that U.S. hospitals with emergency-room services must treat anyone who requires care, including illegal aliens" (Colorado Alliance for Immigration Reform).

Anchor Baby. That's right, anchor baby. The 14th Amendment to the U.S. Constitution reads in part, "All persons born or naturalized in the United States, and subject to the jurisdiction thereof, are citizens of the United States and the State wherein they reside." How do you feel right about now? It's estimated there are over 300,000 anchor babies born each year in the U.S. Thus, illegal alien mothers now add more to the U.S. population each year than immigration from all sources in an average year before 1965. U.S. taxpayers have spent hundreds of millions of dollars on illegal alien patients. Guess who pays? You, me, and every other taxpayer in this country.

Politicians in America have turned their backs on Americans. Even illegal aliens count higher with the American government than native-born, taxpaying, loyal U.S. citizens, who are regarded by their government as nothing but resources to be exploited.... The child is born as an American citizen and, under the 1965 Immigration Act, can be used to facilitate citizenship for the immediate—and ultimately the extended—family.

Disappearing Cash. So long, good bye. "Money transfers from Mexican immigrants working in the United States to relatives back home increased to a record $10 billion in 2002," according to the Pew Hispanic Center in

Washington, D.C. This year's amount is up $800 million from the previous year. This money will not find its way back to America. How many jobs would have been saved if the money would have stayed in America and paid for goods and services right here? Maybe even yours!

Education. The cost of education is on the rise for most American families that unfortunately is not the case for all the illegal aliens. Immigration will account for 96 percent of the increase in the school-age population over the next fifty years. If mass immigration continues, the education of all children in America will continue to be undermined. Education costs will continue to escalate, and the quality of education will continue to decline.

Without school-age immigrants and the children of immigrants, school enrollment would not have risen at all during the past decade. Many states now offer illegal aliens resident tuition, which in most cases is much less than half the tuition amount charged to a non-resident student who is an American citizen and would like to attend a university in another state.

Language. That's right language. We have no obligation whatsoever to teach immigrants or their children the language (Spanish, in almost every case, though there are speakers of 327 other languages living in the United States, according to the 1990 U.S. Census) that was the obligation of their home countries. One scholar, Seymour Martin Lipset, put it this way: The histories of bilingual and bicultural societies that do not assimilate are histories of turmoil, tension, and tragedy. Canada, Belgium, Malaysia, Lebanon—all face crises of national existence in which minorities press for autonomy, if not independence. Pakistan and Cyprus have divided. Nigeria suppressed an ethnic rebellion. France faces difficulties with its Basques, Bretons, and Corsicans. Charles L. King states: "After three to five to seven years of so-called bilingual education, far too many students—most, I dare say—emerge after years essentially illiterate in English."

A common language is the basis, the foundation, for national cultural identity, an identity essential to national unity in any country. A nation is much more than a place on a map. It is a state of mind, a shared vision, and a recognition that we are all in this together. "A nation needs a common language as it needs a common currency," said Seymour Martin Lipset. "America took in many races, religions, and nationalities and made them one nation. Let us be careful with our metaphors. It is a significant asset for an individual to be bilingual, but a path of conflict and tension to have a bilingual nation". Says Richard D. Lamm who is former governor of Colorado said. "The Southwest and, to a lesser extent, the whole nation are in danger of becoming a bilingual nation without debate or forethought. This seems to me to be a grave mistake. I look around the world in vain for an example of where bilingual nations live in peace with themselves. You need to pay close attention to this and take action to stop any attempt at teaching a second language as anything other than an elective language". **Oh, by the way, no nation ever has—that's right, not one ever.**

IRS Giving Cover to Illegal Aliens. You knew it, right? Come on, you knew it. You do now. According to the Center for Immigration Studies, IRS identification for illegal aliens is in fact real and presents a clear danger to all Americans. This identification is known as Individual Tax Identification Numbers(ITINs) and the IRS appears to be blind or indifferent to the fact that they have created an official U.S. tax number that illegal aliens are using as identification, thereby making it easier for them to blend unnoticed into our society, endangering homeland security by issuing ITINs to illegal aliens without adequately ensuring that they are denied to terrorists, criminals on the FBI database, and those under deportation notices. This is about as crazy and irresponsible as it gets: subverted U.S. immigration laws by withholding information from the INS and social security administration about fraudulent activity of illegal aliens. Whose side are they on? Mine? Yours? Not hardly. The most astonishing example is a news release from Fifth Third Bank, headquartered in Ohio. Announcing an initiative to better serve the unique needs of the Hispanic community, Bradlee F. Stamper, president and chief executive officer, proudly boasts, "Our first step—and it's a crucial one—is to start accepting new means of ID for persons otherwise shut out of the U.S. banking system. Starting now, Fifth Third will honor the Matricula Consular Card issued by the government of Mexico, and the Internal Revenue Service's Taxpayer Identification Number as legal identification for immigrants who lack proper identification to open savings and checking accounts." What? I went into a bank in Florida to open a checking account with no success because I did not have the required two picture IDs with me and, of course, my social security number.

Ironically, however, the IRS, a division of the Treasury Department, is simultaneously working to provide illegal aliens with a U.S. government-issued identity number that obviates the need for a social security number. It is called the Individual Taxpayer Identification Number (ITIN). Very little public information about these numbers has been made available, even though the IRS began issuing them in July 1996, and over 5,500,000 of them have been issued. You and I get zip—nothing—without a social security number. This year, the Chicago IRS office and volunteers have issued thousands of ID numbers through workshops and office visits. Almost 300 immigrants, mainly from Mexico but also from the Middle East and Eastern Europe, pack a typical workshop. September 11, 2001, taught us just how important it is to be able to distinguish American citizens and legal foreign residents and visitors from those who have no legal right to be in our country. No security measure is foolproof, but safer is safer. The American people have a right to expect that their government is systematically shutting down any impediments that threaten the integrity of our identity documents.

Matrícula Consular, or Mexican identification card issued by the Mexican government. Bet you didn't know anything about this little beauty. This summer, Indianapolis and seven other Midwestern cities started accepting an identity card issued by the Mexican government, offering Mexicans who are here illegally a startlingly new sense of legitimacy. In Indianapolis, immigrants carrying the matrícula card can apply for building licenses and permits to drive taxis and operate vending carts. **Even if they are here illegally.** The shift has been accompanied by a rising outcry, particularly among some Republicans in Congress, who argue that the widening acceptance of the card is creating a de facto amnesty for illegal immigrants. In March 2002, only a handful of cities and banks recognized the matrícula card, Mexican officials say. Today, more than 100 cities, 900 police departments, 100 financial institutions, and thirteen states, including Indiana, New Mexico, and Utah, accept the cards, which carry the bearer's photo, name, and address, and are issued by Mexican consulates to Mexicans regardless of their immigration status. Emboldened by the changing climate, Mr. Montes de Oca recently carried his card into the red brick offices of National City Bank, which started wooing undocumented immigrants with matrícula cards last year.

Within minutes, he had his first checking account and debit card. "It makes me feel good to see the matrícula accepted in so many places," said Mr. Montes de Oca, twenty-nine, who was rejected when he tried to open a bank account last year because he lacked a social security number. "This makes me feel welcome." Welcome? This illegal needs to be on the next train back to Mexico. Illegal immigrants who carry the matrícula card still risk deportation and are still barred from working by federal law. They cannot use the card to register to vote, change their immigration status, or to obtain social security numbers or work permits. But they often live more freely in cities that recognize the card. And in several states, possession of a matrícula card is the first step toward a driver's license. Officials at the Federal Bureau of Investigation and Department of Homeland Security say this is worrisome because they believe the card is vulnerable to fraud and misuse by criminals and terrorists, a contention that Mexican and some American officials dispute. Officials at the Federal Bureau of Investigation and Department of Homeland Security say this is worrisome because they believe the card is vulnerable to fraud and misuse by criminals and terrorists, a contention that Mexican and some American official's dispute. Remember these people are here illegally.

Amnesty. You make sure this stops. Yes, you. According to the Census Bureau, there were an estimated 8.7 million illegal aliens living in the United States in 2000; roughly 500,000 are added to their number every year, according to the Migration Policy Institute. The INS also estimates that there are over one million transient illegal aliens here at any given time. The number would be higher, but in 1986 our government gave amnesty to nearly three million illegal aliens, allowing them to become legal members of our society. As millions of illegal aliens are allowed to remain here year after year, pressure begins to rise from immigrant advocates to grant amnesty to them. But this is the equivalent of pardoning criminals en masse because it is easier than capturing them. It encourages further illegal immigration and, by creating new "legal" immigrants out of old illegal ones, adds dramatically to the backlog of relatives abroad who apply for legal admission. Illegal alien amnesty is alive and well living inside the United States Department of Justice. Waivers, withholding removal,OR advocates to grant amnesty to them. But this is the equivalent of pardoning criminals en masse because it is easier than capturing them. It encourages further illegal immigration and, by creating new "legal" immigrants out of old illegal ones, adds dramatically to the backlog of relatives abroad who apply for legal admission. Illegal alien amnesty is alive and well living inside the United States Department of Justice. Waivers, withholding removal, suspension of deportation, are just a few ways illegals extend their stays, hoping for amnesty. I do believe most all Americans welcome immigrants to America based on honest, legal entry into our great land.

Did you know? Naturalization is the process by which U.S. citizenship is conferred upon a foreign citizen or national after he or she fulfills the requirements established by Congress in the Immigration and Nationality Act (INA). The general requirements for administrative naturalization include:

1) A period of legal, continuous residence and physical presence in the United States.

2) Residence in a particular INS district prior to filing.

3) An ability to read, write, and speak English.

4) A knowledge and understanding of U.S. history and government.

5) Good moral character.

6) Attachment to the principles of the U.S. Constitution.

7) Favorable disposition toward the United States.

All naturalization applicants must demonstrate good moral character, attachment, and favorable disposition. The other naturalization requirements may be modified or waived for certain applicants, such as spouses of U.S. citizens.

Solution: first seal all the borders with the military if necessary. Eliminate all banking transactions with out proper, verifiable U.S. immigration status. Now that you know the real story, it's time for you to take action and report illegal aliens. If you're really tired of getting screwed, remember illegal aliens are costing America about ninety billion dollars a year. How many children could we educate? How much medical could we provide? You can use the contact information in this book to report illegal aliens, even suspected illegal aliens. Don't worry about being embarrassed. The report can be anonymous. It's time to turn the heat up. Let the authorities check the alien suspect out. If everyone makes one to three phone calls, we can dramatically change the wrong that is being perpetrated on each one of us and our wonderful land. The answer is to deter further illegal immigration and to tackle the removal of the bulk of the illegal alien population through: improving the security of personal identification systems and linkage of governmental databases on births, deaths, and immigration status; better tracking systems for foreigners here on temporary visas; more available detention space for aliens pending deportation; and a national system for employers to electronically verify employees' work eligibility. Impress upon all politicians the foregoing must change and now. Sources: The Center for Immigration Studies; and Don Huddle's *The Net Costs of Immigration, the INS Statistics Division.* **No IDs of any kind for illegal aliens.**

The following contact information is provided so you can take action by reporting illegal aliens and employers. *<www.imigration.gov/graphics/fieldoffices/index.htm>*

The following is a list of immigration field office telephone numbers. Choose the closest office to the alleged illegal activity. Report employers you suspect are employing illegal immigrants. Report individuals you suspect are illegal aliens. If we all make three phone calls and we write to three politicians, they will have no choice but to stop this madness. **Your action will force the INS to open a case file on the complaint. Good luck and God bless you and America.**

CHAPTER TWO

TAXES

Taxes. People complain but they pay and pay and pay. Let's take a look at just what we are burdened with. Most pay simply out of fear. Pay Tax on your water bill, tax on your light bill, tax on your phone bill, tax, tax, tax. If you take into consideration the total taxes that we Americans pay, we are the highest taxed people in the world. Just why is that?

Then we have the great crowd who should pay and don't. Let's get a very clear understanding of the history of taxes in our great America, or is it legal plunder?

Every nation, democratic or not, taxes its people. Every government needs money to operate and provide some sort of services, along with protection from other countries or people who would otherwise enslave them. The question then becomes how much and who pays. Lady Godiva successfully reduced the tax assessment on her husband, the Earl of Mercia, by riding naked on a white horse through the streets of Coventry. Many of the American taxpayers feel naked or worse at tax time. Throughout history, the collection of taxes has had interesting results. In the year

60 A.D. the Queen of East England rebelled against corrupt tax collectors. The queen succeeded in recruiting 230,000 warriors to fight the war, and when it was over, some 80,000 men had been killed.

In 1369, the reason for the renewal of the 100 Years War between England and France was the rebellion of the nobility against the tax policy of Edward, the Black Prince.

U.S. Tax History. The nation had few taxes in its early history. From 1791 to 1802, the United States government was supported by internal taxes on distilled spirits, carriages, refined sugar, tobacco and snuff, property sold at auction, corporate bonds, and slaves. The high cost of the War of 1812 brought about the nation's first sales taxes on gold, silverware, jewelry, and watches. **In 1817, however, Congress did away with all internal taxes, relying on tariffs on imported goods to provide sufficient funds for running the government.**

In 1862, in order to support the Civil War effort, Congress enacted the nation's first income tax law. It was a forerunner of our modern income tax in that it was based on the principles of graduated, or progressive, taxation and of withholding income at the source. During the Civil War, a person earning from $600 to $10,000 per year paid tax at the rate of 3 percent. Those with incomes of more than $10,000 paid taxes at a higher rate. Additional sales and excise taxes were added, and an "inheritance" tax also made its debut. In 1866, internal revenue collections reached their highest point in the nation's ninety-year history—more than $310 million, an amount not reached again until 1911.

The Act of 1862 established the office of Commissioner of Internal Revenue. The commissioner was given the power to assess, levy, and collect taxes, and the right to enforce the tax laws through seizure of property and income, and through prosecution. His powers and authority remain very much the same today.

In 1868, Congress again focused its taxation efforts on tobacco and distilled spirits and eliminated the income tax in 1872. It had a short-lived revival in 1894 and 1895. In the latter year, the U.S. Supreme Court decided that the income tax was unconstitutional because it was not apportioned among the states in conformity with the Constitution.

In 1913, the 16th Amendment to the Constitution made the income tax a permanent fixture in the U.S. tax system. The amendment gave Congress legal authority to tax income, and resulted in a revenue law that taxed incomes of both individuals and corporations. In fiscal year 1918, annual internal revenue collections for the first time passed the billion-dollar mark, rising to $5.4 billion by 1920. With the advent of World War II, employment increased, as did tax collections—to $7.3 billion. The withholding tax on wages was introduced in 1943, and was instrumental in increasing the number of taxpayers to 60 million and tax collections to $43 billion by 1945.

In 1981, Congress enacted the largest tax cut in U.S. history, approximately $750 billion over six years. The tax reduction, however, was partially offset by two tax acts, in 1982 and 1984 that attempted to raise approximately $265 billion.

On October 22, 1986, President Reagan signed into law the Tax Reform Act of 1986, one of the most far-reaching reforms of the United States tax system since the adoption of the income tax. In an attempt to remain revenue neutral, the act called for a $120 billion increase in business taxation and a corresponding decrease in individual taxation over a five-year period.

Following what seemed to be a yearly tradition of new tax acts that began in 1986, the Revenue Reconciliation Act of 1990 was signed into law on November 5, 1990. As with the '87, '88, and '89 acts, the 1990 act, while providing a number of substantive provisions, was small in comparison with the 1986 act. The emphasis of the 1990 act was on increased taxes for the wealthy.

On August 10, 1993, President Clinton signed the Revenue Reconciliation Act of 1993 into law. The act's purpose was to reduce by approximately $496 billion the federal deficit that would otherwise accumulate in fiscal years 1994 through 1998.

On August 5, 1997, President Clinton signed the Taxpayer Relief Act of 1997. The act included $152 billion in tax cuts, a cut in capital-gains tax for individuals, a $500 per child tax credit, estate tax relief, tax incentives for education, and a host of revenue-raising and tax-simplification provisions.

On June 7, 2001, President George W. Bush signed the Economic Growth and Tax Relief Reconciliation Act of 2001. The act included a variety of tax cuts and offered benefits to a broad range of taxpayers through relief provisions that included: married couples; families with children, who would receive tax cuts to help pay for education, childcare, and other expenses; single mothers; and seniors. The act also included tax cuts that completely eliminated the entire income tax liability for some families.

President Bush signed the Job Creation and Workers Assistance Act of 2002 on March 9, 2002. The act's primary focus was to provide tax relief to businesses with a 30 percent expensing provision on the value of capital assets. The act also included a thirteen-week extension on unemployment insurance and tax breaks for taxpayers affected by the September 11 2001 terrorist attacks. Overall, the act projected tax relief of $41.9 billion over the 2003–2012 period.

President Bush signed another tax-relief package on May 28, 2003. The Jobs and Growth Tax Relief and Reconciliation Act of 2003 accelerated most of the tax-relief provisions associated with 2001's Economic Growth and Tax Relief Reconciliation Act, most of which would have been phased in beginning in 2005 under the 2001 law. The law also lowered the tax rate **on dividends** and capital gains to 15 percent, and increased the expensing provision related to the Job Creation and Workers Assistance Act of 2002 to 50 percent from 30 percent. *Source: Scott Moody, senior economist, the Tax Foundation.*

Who pays? Below is an analysis of Congressional Budget Office (CBO) report entitled "Preliminary Estimates of Effective Tax Rates" (07-Sept-1999). The raw numbers can be scrutinized here: *<http://www.cbo.gov/showdoc.cfm ?index=1545&from=4&sequence=0>*

All I did was try to make heads or tails of the data by plotting it and extracting the most salient data. The *income tax burden* is defined simply as **who pays** U.S. income taxes in the form of individual and corporate income taxes, payroll taxes, and federal excise taxes. Based on this information, the following conclusions clearly emerge. An enormous percentage of taxes are paid by a minority of Americans:

The top 1 percent of taxpayers pays 29 percent of all taxes.

The top 5 percent of taxpayers pays 50 percent of all taxes.

Our tax system is not so much progressive as it is confiscatory—Frederic Bastiat called this phenomenon **"legal plunder."** A *progressive tax* is based on the premise that those with more income can afford to pay more taxes, and conversely, those with little or no income should pay no tax. However, a quick look at graph 1A below shows that the U.S. tax system has become far more than progressive. Fully half the taxpayers contribute almost nothing in individual income taxes.

The top 1 percent of income earners (comprising about 1 million families) earns about 15 percent of the total income earned by all wage earners in the United States, yet **they pay almost 30 percent of all individual income taxes**.

Furthermore, the top 1 percent is shouldering a roughly 50 percent higher proportion of the overall income tax burden than they did in 1977.

The argument most often used against tax breaks is that they benefit only the wealthy. It is clear from even a cursory look at the numbers below that **the "wealthy" will receive the majority of any income tax reduction because they pay a disproportionately huge percentage of the income taxes!** To structure a tax break such that those in upper-income brackets are excluded would constitute nothing more than a transfer of wealth from those who have it to those who don't (i.e., legal plunder).

Raw Data: Share of Individual Income Tax (in %)

Income Category	1977	1979	1981	1983	1985	1987	1989	1991	1993	1995	1999 (Projected)
Highest 20%	68	67	66	68	68	72	72	72	75	77	79
Fourth 20%	20	20	20	20	19	18	17	18	17	16	16
Middle 20%	10	10	10	10	9	8	9	9	8	8	7
Second 20%	3	4	4	3	3	3	3	2	2	1	1
Lowest 20%	0	0	0	0	0	0	-1	-1	-1	-2	-2
All Families	100	100	100	100	100	100	100	100	100	100	100
Top 1%	20	19	17	20	21	24	24	23	27	29	29
Top 5%	38	37	36	38	39	43	44	42	46	49	50
Top 10%	50	50	49	51	52	56	56	55	59	61	63

Source: Sugi Sorensen and Stephen Cobb, "Preliminary Estimates of Effective Tax Rates," Congressional Budget Office (September 7, 1999): http://www.cbo.gov/showdoc. cfm?index=1545&from=4&sequence=0>, last revised April 17, 2000.

You and I need to stop listing to the lies politicians are feeding us day in and day out. It becomes crystal clear who pays the majority of the taxes in this country and it is not the poor. What would they pay it with anyway?

Now come the corporations. Vol. V No. 34 December 12, 2000

Many of the biggest corporations in the U.S. pay few or no taxes on their profits, according to a recent study. The study by the Institute on Taxation and Economic Policy (ITEP) on the 250 biggest corporations in the U.S. found that these corporations paid an average 20.1 percent in taxes on their profits from 1996-98—nearly half of the rate of 35 percent required by federal law.

Had all of the companies paid the rate required by law, they would have collectively owed $257 billion. Instead, assorted tax breaks lowered that figure to $159 billion. In fact, some of these corporations even got refund checks from the U.S. Treasury. Forty-one companies paid less than nothing in federal income taxes in at least one year from 1996 to 1998, according to the report. In those years, the companies reported a total of $25.8 billion in pre-tax U.S. profits. But rather than pay the appropriate $9 billion in federal income taxes, these companies instead enjoyed tax refunds of $3.2 billion. Almost half of the tax breaks went to just twenty-five companies, each getting more than a billion-dollar tax benefit. The big winner was General Electric, with $6.9 billion in tax breaks over the three years the study looked at. Cisco Systems, the second most valuable company in the U.S., paid no federal income taxes in the latest fiscal year, despite their $2.7 billion in net earnings. In another example, Texaco reported $3.4 billion in profits and received $304 million in tax rebates. In fact, oil companies, as a group, were the lowest-taxed industry, with an effective federal tax rate of 12.3 percent. Only one industry, publishing, paid an effective tax level of 30 percent. How do these companies get away with it? They use a variety of means to lower their federal income taxes, including depreciation write-offs, tax credits for things like research and oil drilling, and tax breaks for doing business in Puerto Rico. For example, GE continues to slash its tax bills every year through its leasing activities that essentially buy tax breaks from companies that have more than they can use. The fastest-growing tax break for U.S. companies is the use of stock options. By taking the difference between what an employee pays for a stock and what it's worth, 233 of 250 companies lowered their taxes from stock options by a total of $25.8 billion over the last three years, the study found. **It is unfair for multi-billion-dollar companies to escape all income taxes.** Individual Americans must pay their taxes, and these corporations should too. For more information, contact Keith Ashdown at (202) 546-8500 x110.

The Ugly Facts. In the year 2000, the 1040 form was seventy lines long and had 117 pages of instructions. Individuals and businesses waste nearly $200 billion a year filing their taxes. We bear this burden through higher prices and lower wages. The IRS prints some 280 instruction forms to explain how to complete nearly 480 tax returns. The tax code is so large that each year the IRS mails enough pages of forms and instructions to circle the Earth nearly twenty-eight times. The number of IRS employees has more than doubled in the last thirty years. Half of all filers hire someone else to do their taxes.

Russia's Flat Tax Reform. Russia switched to a 13 percent flat tax and tax revenues increased. That's right, revenues increased. Since January 1, 2001, Russians have enjoyed a 13 percent flat tax.

Even the old Russian system was simpler than ours, with three tax rates—12, 20, and 30 percent. The U.S. has six—6, 10, 15, 27, 30, 35, and 38.6 percent, the last of which takes hold at $307,500 for married couples filing jointly. The majority of Russian taxpayers don't need to file forms. The 13 percent rate has exceeded expectations in terms of revenue, as real ruble revenue increased 28 percent three years ago; tax revenue equaled 9 to 10 percent of Russian gross domestic product. By last November that had grown to 16 percent as result following the Laffer Curve: **lower marginal tax rates produce higher revenues.** The new system has also greatly reduced the underground economy, where people were paid in goods rather than cash to facilitate tax evasion. In other pro-market moves, President Vladimir Putin has signed legislation to cut the corporate tax rate from 35 to 24 percent. The Kremlin may also offer Russians privately invested social security accounts, much as President Bush wants for Americans. As one observer has noted, V. I. Lenin, analyzing all this from his dacha in hell, must be stroking his beard in utter bewilderment. Source: Deroy Murdock, "Even Russia Realized the Wisdom of a Flat Tax," *Dallas Morning News*, March 4, 2002.

In 2001, Americans spent 6.4 billion hours filling out tax forms for the government.

Switching to a flat tax would make it simple to pay taxes, saving everyone time and money. Under a flat tax, filing taxes would take mere minutes, and decreasing compliance costs would improve the economy—all of those billions of hours we spend filing taxes could be put to productive use. **Go ahead and compute your flat tax below,** keeping in mind the time that you save in filling out a simple form, and that economic growth will improve your income situation immensely. Go to *<www.cse.org>* to use the flat tax form to compute your tax obligation. Your tax liability will be less.

Liberals ought to love a flat tax! When you tax everyone at the same rate, the rich pay much more in taxes than the middle class and the poor. With three times the income, you pay three times the tax, and so on. And beyond this, a flat tax is in its own way "progressive." If you make three times the income, you pay three times the tax. And thanks to a generous family allowance, even with a flat rate a family making $33,300 a year would pay no federal income tax, while a family making $200,000 a year would end up, because of the $33,300 exemption, paying 14 percent of its income. Indeed, about 20 million Americans would be dropped from the tax roles altogether. What's not for a liberal to love? By sweeping away all the special-interest loopholes, the flat tax will show us how much money government is really costing us. By eliminating the present tax code's incessant social engineering and economic tinkering, the flat tax is more honest, shifting power from politicians to their citizens when it comes to making financial judgments. The flat tax is pro-growth; planting the seeds for needed rises in output and wages. The chief cause of our long-stagnant wages in the U.S. is our anemic saving rate, and the chief cause of our low saving rate is today's policy of taxing savings twice, once when a dollar is earned, and then again when it produces a return. The flat tax wipes out this perverse bias against saving; savings will rise, the nation's pool of capital will grow, workers will be better equipped and trained, and output will expand, leading to bigger paychecks.

So there you have it: simplicity, honesty, growth, and fairness—four reasons people should love a flat tax. But allow me to address some of the concerns that have been raised.

The first comes from the class-warfare crowd. Our plan taxes investment income at exactly the same rate it taxes wages; but what it doesn't do is tax it twice. Today a dollar of corporate earnings is taxed at the business level, and taxed again when it's paid out as a dividend. Our bill, by way of contrast, would tax every dollar of business-generated income at the business level, once and only once. To suggest as some have that our plan does not tax investment income is a misrepresentation of the plan.

A second area of concern is the elimination of the home mortgage interest deduction, which some critics assume will hurt the real-estate industry. But eliminating the mortgage interest deduction won't hurt the industry nearly so much as lower interest rates will help it.

Interestingly, a recent poll showed that by a three-to-one margin, homeowners said they'd be willing to forego the mortgage interest deduction if the loss was offset by a reduction of their tax bills in similar amounts.

A third concern comes from our conservative friends who are worried that charities may suffer without a continued tax deduction for philanthropic giving. But in truth, almost half of charitable contributions today are not even claimed as tax deductions. When President Reagan cut the top marginal rate from 70 percent to 28 percent, charitable giving became much less valuable for tax purposes, and yet charitable giving didn't drop, but actually doubled.

What, then, is the "Freedom and Fairness Restoration Act?" It's an overdue plan so simple you could do your taxes on a postcard, but it's more than that—it's a vision of what America can be again—literally a formula for rejuvenating our economy, freeing our entrepreneurial talent and reviving family incomes that for too long have remained stagnant.

"And who knows? It might just restore people's willingness to trust their government, which is why I believe there's a flat tax is in America's future". Said Congressman Dick Armey (R-TX)

You and I need to act now and support tax reform. Make those phone calls and write the letters send the email. Go to your computer, look up flat tax organizations, and support them. Please act now and support your own financial future. Good luck to us all.

CHAPTER THREE

EDUCATION

"No Child Left Behind." How did our children get left behind to begin with? The United States has one of the highest student dropout rates in the world. We have classrooms that are overcrowded; lack discipline, and about 30 percent of the students are not on grade level in English reading and writing skills. We have teachers who are overworked, underpaid, and dropping out of the profession of education. What is the history of our educational progress in the United States? You're going to be very surprised to find that many of the problems we face today have existed in our country before.

No Child Left Behind consists of federal requirements for every state to have a federally approved plan for ensuring that all students are proficient in reading and mathematics by 2013-14. State plans for holding schools and districts accountable for the academic performance of all students are, arguably, at the heart of the No Child Left Behind Act of 2001, the reauthorization of the Elementary and Secondary Education Act that the president signed into law a year ago on January 8 2002 The announcement came on the congressional deadline day for the U.S. Department of Education to review and approve each state's plan; 120 days after the states were required to submit their plans. In the past few months, the department had accepted plans for thirty-three states, plus the District of Columbia and Puerto Rico. Seventeen more were given the go-ahead the morning of the June 10 deadline.

"Since the plans themselves, and the basis for approving them, are not yet widely available or publicly available, it's hard to know what to make of it," said Michael Cohen, the president of Achieve, a Washington-based organization that promotes standards-based education.

"If we're going to have accountability up and down the line," he continued, "then it's really important for the Department of Education review, and approval, and judgment of these plans to be 100 percent transparent."

Mr. Cohen, who was an assistant secretary of education in the Clinton administration, added, "The fact that they have gotten all fifty states to approve either means that they're awfully and quickly persuasive in getting states to do exactly what the law requires, or they've given states a lot of slack in meeting the requirements."

Every state will receive a follow-up letter from Eugene W. Hickok, the undersecretary of education, that could include a "clarifying statement or two," said Ron Tomalis, his chief of staff. But, added Mr. Tomalis, who has been designated to oversee the department's office of elementary and secondary education, "I don't anticipate any issue in a follow-up letter that has not already been discussed and negotiated with a state."

States also are free to amend their plans, which some schools chiefs said they might do after seeing what got the nod in other states. But any changes would require department approval.

You guessed it: states are already challenging the standards and the requirements of the federal law. "I think there's more flexibility than they told us several months ago to expect," said Tom Horne, the state schools chief in Arizona, "and we're hoping to use that to avoid the over-identification of failing schools." Over-identification of failing schools: that's exactly what the law is supposed to identify and correct. Even states that didn't get everything they wanted said the negotiations had been fair.

Federal officials rejected Michigan's proposal to exempt students with limited English skills from taking state tests if they've been enrolled in U.S. schools for less than three years. Instead, the state plans to amend a standardized test that uses a simpler level of English than its state exams to measure the reading and math skills of students who lack the fluency to take part in the regular assessment.

"At the end of the day, we had to capitulate to what the law was," said Thomas D. Watkins, Michigan's superintendent of public instruction. "I don't like stopping at stop signs either, but there are consequences if you don't." No kidding. Here we go, already lowering the standards to look better when in reality we are not better but worse. When are Americans going to get off the shortcut-to-everything program and face the realities of hard work? You do not get everything you want in ninety seconds. You definitely will not excel by lowering the requirements or standards.

"Special Circumstance." Although the department did not grant any waivers, it did raise a few eyebrows.

For example, it approved Iowa's plan, even though the state has no statewide academic-content standards and intends to use two off-the-shelf, norm-referenced tests to measure progress. Federal officials had earlier stressed that states using such tests must augment them, as necessary, to better reflect state standards. "States have worked extremely hard at the highest levels to address these plans and to implement 'adequate yearly progress' in their unique state context," said Scott R. Palmer, a lawyer with the Washington firm of Nixon Peabody, which has provided technical assistance to several states. "I think it's been a learning curve for the states and for the department, frankly." Wait a minute; if one plus one equals two in one state does it equal three or maybe four in another state? Evidently it does, but it really doesn't, does it?

The answer to this problem is a standardization of materials and texts and tests throughout the entire country, in every state and every county and city. Many other countries use standard materials and testing for a true measure of where they really are concerning educating there population. Without standard test materials for everyone, and everyone taking the same test, you have gauged nothing and arrived at nothing. If you have gauged nothing and you are without information for planning, or developing a real productive solution, you will arrive exactly where America is now: very low on the list of progressive countries in educating its people.

Continued Concern. In a speech President Bush asserted that the federal government is "meeting our obligations," noting that his proposed federal budget for the next fiscal year would boost education funding to $53.1 billion, an increase of nearly $11 billion since he took office. But, he warned, "It's also important to recognize that pouring money into systems that do not teach and refuse to change will not help children." Let me show you an all-too-accurate graph that proves this. This graph doesn't say that SAT scores have *increased above* the funding rate per student.

It doesn't say that the SAT scores have *kept pace* with the funding rate per student.

It says that SAT scores have *dropped 71 percent* **in spite of all the funding!**

Is there a more significant, scientific correlation proving that federal funding **CAUSES** lower SAT scores?

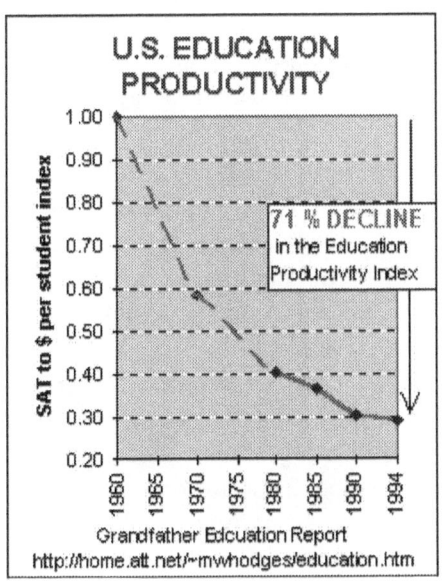

Mr. Horne of Florida contended that the federal money is adequate. "Of course everyone wants more money," he said. But he said that, while Florida isn't starting from scratch like some other states, that's because it has invested substantial money in its accountability system. Then Mr. Horne needs to explain why Florida is number forty-seven out fifty states.

The big concern is that states not establish "dual" systems—one for schools receiving Title I money and one for everyone else—as had been true for many states under the 1994 version of the ESEA. Groups such as the Citizens' Commission on Civil Rights will be tracking that issue closely. That's one very big reason why our entire educational system has failed for the most part: we have allowed special-interest this and that to disrupt standardization of testing. Oh by the way, you save your redundant rhetoric concerning the differences between the poor the rich and the foreign students. You must teach the same material to all and give the same test to all to arrive at any meaningful statistics to make any real predetermined progress. Get it?

Unresolved Issues. States are still struggling to interpret some of the more contentious of the accountability provisions, particularly those related to students with limited command of English or with disabilities. State leaders have expressed concerns about testing the reading and math skills of students in English while they are still mastering the language. States are also worried that once students become proficient in English, they will move out of the limited-English subgroup, so that it will be hard for the subgroup ever to meet its performance targets. Who cares if the subgroup ever does anything other than getting students on grade level with English skills? Isn't that what they are supposed to be doing?

Some states—such as Illinois, South Carolina, and Tennessee—are taking advantage of flexibility in the federal statute and will count the scores of students with limited English in that subgroup until they score at the "proficient" level on state tests of English adeptness for two or three years in a row. Now were talking. Texas will include students in the limited-English subgroup until they score at the "met standard" level on the state's English reading test for two consecutive years after entering a regular, all-English instructional program. California will include students in that subgroup until they've attained the "proficient" level on the state test in English/language arts for three years running. Okay then, now were going somewhere positive. In the public school system that is.

Universities Seeking Home schooled Students. That's right home schooled. What is home schooling and why are the leading universities actually inviting homeschooled students to apply to there school?

Natural Talent and Classroom Conflicts. Thomas Edison's short stay in the classroom was a disaster. His mother pulled him out and gave him a workshop so he could develop his natural talent at his own pace; she was not concerned about academics. You know the rest of the story. What if he had lived in today's type of government-subsidized housing unit? Being a frustrated young man, he would turn to crime and drugs, then spend his life in prison, all because he could not find his true talent and/or an outlet to develop it, if found.

Michael Lameyer

Posted 9/2/2003 7:57 PM

Support for home-schoolers can pay off for all students

As 47 million children return to public schools, some 2 million are staying home to get their instruction. In nearly every state, the number of children being educated in their homes is rising about 10% a year.

The growth reflects a vast broadening in the types of families that embrace home schooling. The stereotype of home-schoolers as religious separatists or the offspring of New Age seekers has not been true for years. Now, though, local home-schooling organizations report that about 10% of their families are black or Hispanic.

The growing diversity among families that teach their children themselves is linked to the spreading popularity of the school choice movement. Parents like having the power to choose the educational setting that best serves their children's needs.

Yet instead of accepting—even welcoming—the valuable role home school supporters can play in increasing choices, too many traditional educators are setting up roadblocks. Some states impose excessive paperwork demands on home schooling parents, even when their children appear to be flourishing academically. Many school districts deny home-schooled children the opportunity to participate in music and sports activities at local schools.

Such moves can needlessly deprive public schools of valuable alliances with taxpayers and advocates of quality education.

Several proven ways can help more states and school districts reach out to home schooling parents. Among them:

•Funding online teaching. The Florida Virtual School is a public school that conducts classes over the Internet. Students include not only home schoolers but also students looking for courses their local schools don't offer, or more flexible class schedules.

• Reducing burdensome paperwork. Maine did so in May as one of several states that acceded to home schooling parents' requests to be treated more like families in private schools. In recent years, Oregon, Arkansas, and Arizona have loosened onerous rules aimed at homes schoolers.

•Letting home schoolers join school activities. In July, the Pennsylvania House of Representatives passed a bill requiring the state's 501 school districts to open sports teams and other extracurricular activities to homes schoolers. The measure, which goes to the state senate this fall, reflects a national trend granting home-schooled students use of some public-school services.

Those critical of home schooling argue that parents often fall short as competent teachers. To date, though, no evidence demonstrates a significant problem of home-schooled children receiving poor educations. In fact, research suggests home schooling can be very effective.

Families choosing home schooling provide the close parental involvement that students need to succeed academically. Supporting that choice benefits children, their parents, and local school districts.

Editorial: Back-to-School
Washington Times
September 1, 2003
by J. Michael Smith
HSLDA President

It's that time of year. Back to school season when parents scramble to supply their children with all the latest school accessories. After the long summer break, many parents no doubt are relieved to send their children packing and return to the school schedule. Parents will be asking some or all of the following questions during this season: How much academic progress will my child make this year compared to last? Will my child grow in character and maturity? Will my child have good teachers who will provide challenging academic courses? **Is the school providing a safe environment where my child can learn without negative peer pressure?**

In today's world, more and more parents are finding it increasingly difficult to answer these questions to their satisfaction. It is one of the reasons why the school choice movement, which includes homeschooling, has been growing so rapidly over the past fifteen years.

The back-to-school season is the time many parents make a choice about their children's education. Large numbers of parents are desperate to find alternatives to failing public schools. Homeschooling is not the only education choice, but it is the fastest-growing one. The best estimates find that homeschoolers have reached the 2 million mark, which is the equivalent of the entire New Jersey school system. Homeschooling is growing at an average of 15 percent per year.

Parents who already have chosen homeschooling avoid the back-to-school drama because most operate on the basis of continuous learning. **Many homeschool families follow a four weeks on/one week off schedule. This type of schedule helps children keep a constant pace in their academic studies rather than taking an extended break where children can fall out of the habit of learning.** Of course many families succeed with different schedules, which is one of the advantages of homeschooling. There's no need to follow someone else's schedule. You can make your own to suit your family's needs.

Homeschool families often cite flexibility as one of the key advantages. Families experience success with a variety of methods. This is to be expected because each homeschool program is tailored to the child's needs rather than the one-size-fits-all instruction of the schools. One-on-one tutoring will always have a significant advantage over 30:1 or 25:1 ratios. It's parents who are in the best position to know what their child needs and how their child learns.

Parents can confidently answer yes to the questions they have to face during the back-to-school season by choosing homeschooling. Will my child have good teachers? The answer is that parents are the child's best teacher. Who knows your child better than yourself? Also, parents will be able to spend the time necessary to advance their child socially and academically.

Where is the best learning environment for your child? One of the main reasons parents choose homeschooling is the elevated levels of crime, drugs, and other negative peer influences present in public schools. The home is the safest learning environment, where a child can pursue his own interests at his own pace. Will the child develop character and maturity? The answer is yes again. The homeschool environment provides far greater time for interaction with other adults. When a child becomes an adult he will spend the majority of the time surrounded by other adults. Conversely, a child in the typical school setting will mostly interact with his own peer group. Homeschoolers develop the habits they need in adult life at an earlier age. Who do you want influencing your child, you as the parent or your child's peers?

The back-to-school season is a time of choosing. Which path will you take? Increasingly, parents are saying they want alternatives to institutional schools, and many are making the ultimate school choice and turning their own homes into schools. For those interested in finding out more about home schooling, go to www.youcanhomeschool.org you can get more valuable information on how to get started.

In the broad spectrum of history, home education is nothing new—parents have been teaching their children for centuries. American history is full of men and women who were taught at home, from colonial patriot Patrick Henry to President John Quincy Adams to inventor Thomas Edison.

However, in today's world of fast-paced technology and government regulation, the rebirth of home education has raised more than a few eyebrows. "How can ordinary parents hope to do as well as the educational experts?" critics ask. Others wonder, "Who are these families? What drives them to choose such an unusual lifestyle?" Every year, the experts-know-better-than-parents philosophy finds its way into legislation designed to increase the regulation of home education. Similarly, the lack of knowledge about those who home school finds its way into public perception of the home schooling movement.

Clearly, answers are needed. In 1998, Home School Legal Defense Association commissioned the largest research study to date of home education in America. Conducted by Dr. Lawrence Rudner of the ERIC Clearinghouse on Assessment and Evaluation, the study involved seven times as many home schooling families as any previous study of its kind. The families compiled the data from the achievement test scores of 20,760 students in 11,930 families, along with background questionnaires submitted.

Unlike any previous study, families chose to participate before they knew their children's test scores. Thus, the possibility of reporting higher scores while leaving lower scores unreported was considerably diminished. Another factor that sets the Rudner study apart is the fact that all students took the same tests. Did you hear that? The same test, the Iowa Test of Basic Skills (ITBS) for grades K–8, and the Tests of Achievement and Proficiency (TAP) for grades 9–12, both published by the Riverside Publishing Company. Furthermore, this research, conducted by an impartial third party whose own children are enrolled in public school, avoids the criticism of pro-home school bias leveled against previous studies, which were conducted by proponents of home education. Home schooling thrives on individuality, and the home-education movement daily becomes more diverse. These factors make it difficult to determine whether achievement test scores are truly the best demonstration of home school achievement, and whether the families involved in the Rudner study are an exact representation of the movement as a whole. However, both the academic and demographic findings of this study do much to provide us with an informative portrait of modern home education in America.

Academic and demographic information from the largest national study of home schooled students.
How do home schoolers measure up?

Average Home School Test Scores			
Grade	Number of students studied	PERCENTILE RANK		
		Reading	Language	Math
1	1,504	88	82	81
2	2,153	89	80	85
3	2,876	83	82	78
4	2,625	83	67	76
5	2,564	83	69	76
6	2,420	82	73	76
7	2,087	87	77	79
8	1,801	86	79	76
9	1,164	82	77	68
10	775	89	84	72
11	317	84	83	68
12	66	92	85	66

Home school students do exceptionally well when compared with the nationwide average. In every subject and at every grade level of the ITBS and TAP batteries, home school students scored significantly higher than their public and private school counterparts (figure 1).

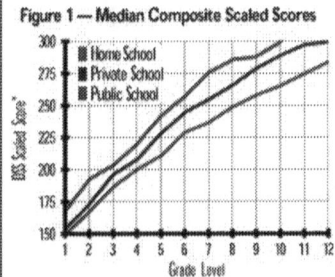

Figure 1 — Median Composite Scaled Scores

Because home education allows each student to progress at his or her own rate, almost one in four home school students (24.5 percent) are enrolled one or more

47

grades above age level (figure 2). It should be noted that home school scores were analyzed according to the student's enrolled grade rather than according to the student's age level. In other words, a ten-year-old home school student enrolled in the fifth grade would have been compared to other students in the fifth grade, rather than to his age-level peers in the fourth grade. Thus, the demonstrated achievement of home schoolers is somewhat conservative.

Figure 2 — Enrolled Grade Compared to Age of Home School Student

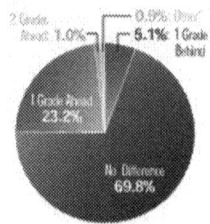

On average, home school students in grades one to four perform one grade level higher than their public and private school counterparts. The achievement gap begins to widen in grade five; by eighth grade the average home school student performs four grade levels above the national average (figure 3).

Figure 3 — Home School Median Scaled Scores (and Corresponding Grade Equivalent Scores*)

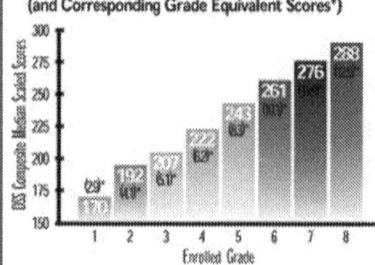

Another significant finding is that students who have been home schooled their entire academic lives have the highest scholastic achievement. The difference becomes especially pronounced during the higher grades, suggesting that students who remain in home school throughout their high school years continue to flourish in that environment (figure 4).

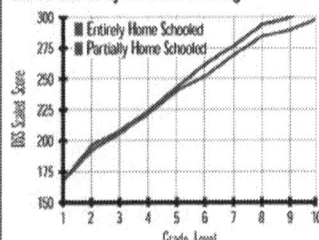

Figure 4 — Home Schooled Median Scaled Scores by Academic Setting

Differences were also found among home school students when they were classified by the amount of money spent on education, their family's income, their parents' education, and their television viewing. However, it should be noted that home school students in every category scored significantly higher than the national average.

Figure 5 — Home School Percentile Rankings Based on Gender

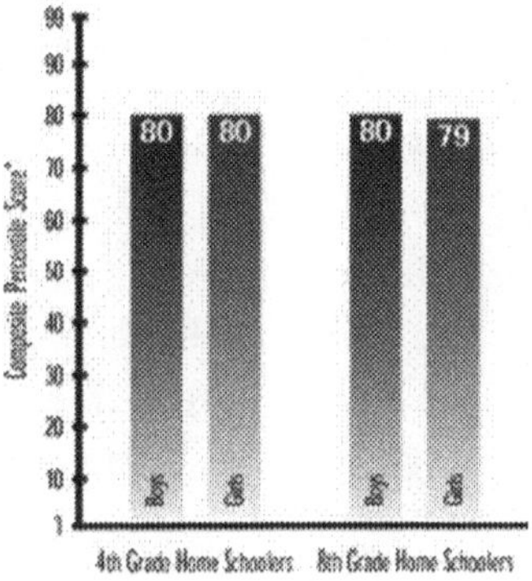

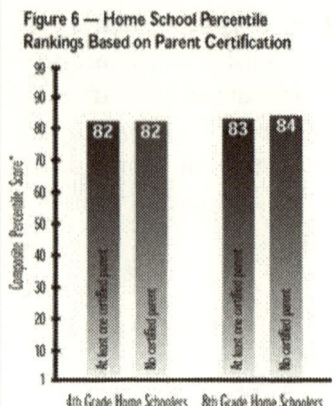

Figure 6 — Home School Percentile Rankings Based on Parent Certification

No meaningful difference was found among home school students when classified by gender (figure 5). Significantly, there was also no difference found according to whether or not a parent was certified to teach (figure 6). For those who would argue that only certified teachers should be allowed to teach their children at home, these findings suggest that such a requirement would not meaningfully affect student achievement.

FOOTNOTES

FIGURE 1: * Developmental Standard Score (DSS) is the test publisher's (Riverside) scale used for public, private, and home school students to describe each student's location on an achievement continuum that spans grades K through 12. The DSS scale varies by subject area. Scale capped at 300 because differences at the top are inappropriately exaggerated.

FIGURE 2: * "Other" includes all those enrolled more than two grades ahead or more than one grade behind.

FIGURE 3: * Grade Equivalent Scores (GES) are a reference point for interpreting DSS scores. A GES approximates a child's development in terms of grade and month within grade. (For example: A DSS composite score of 170 can be viewed as the typical DSS score earned by students in the ninth month of the second grade or a GES score of 2.9.)

FIGURE 4: * Scale capped at 300 because differences at the top are inappropriately exaggerated.

FIGURE 5: * Composite Percentile Score refers to the percentile corresponding to the mean composite scaled score.

FIGURE 6: * Composite Percentile Score refers to the percentile corresponding to the mean composite scaled score.

Home schooling is here to stay! Now you know why universities are looking for these independent performers. Never would have guessed, would you?

Project-Based Education.
http://www.motivation-tools.com/youth/project_education.html
Project Based Education

An alternative for academic based education.
What do these people have in common? Benjamin Franklin, Abraham Lincoln, Thomas Edison, Henry Ford, The Wright Brothers', Frank Sinatra, and Elvis Presley. They educated themselves with self-motivated projects. Academics was a byproduct that was acquired as needed and at the level needed to achieve their goal. These people were in conflict with classroom education. They succeeded because they discovered their natural talent and built a career based on that discovery. Education that is based on projects is highly motivating and is man's natural learning process. The discovery and opportunity to develop natural talent inspires

a productive lifestyle. Project based education can give students that opportunity.

The Project Based Education program is based on what interests and motivates the student. Because the instructor cannot customize lesson plans for each student, he must implement student responsibility. It becomes the student's responsibility to develop and research projects and develop a plan of action. The instructor acts as a coach or facilitator. Instructors take an interest in students' projects instead of students having to take an interest in topics handed down by administrators.

Today's education system is based on academics and tests are used to gauge progress. A high percent of students are in tune with the current system, but there will always be the 30% who cannot associate classroom instruction with the real world. This is especially true for students with creative minds that are searching for alternatives. Project based education would solve this problem.

Projects require a goal where students must search for a method, acquire skills and knowledge, accept failure and bounce back from it, and keep trying until the goal is achieved. They learn through experiences, more important, they learn how to research and apply knowledge. Success is measured by the complexity of the project and the ability to finish it. This type of education motivates one to learn more about the world we live in while creating a lifetime love to learn. The laws' of nature is the motivator and instructor. Positive self-esteem is one of the many by-products.

There are three types of projects:
Class Motivated - In this case, the instructor initiates the project and sets the goal. Competition type projects are

effective. Some students may need to be taught the art of project development before they are assigned to smaller groups.

Team Motivated - A team of 2 to 5 members agree on a common interest project. With teams, the opportunity to share knowledge has a powerful influence on team members. It motivates others to find ways to contribute information or skills. When things go wrong, strong team members can support and encourage the weaker ones. Support from associates is a powerful force. Peer pressure motivates all to excel.

Self-Motivated - Some students are independent, strong-willed and have a natural talent with projects. They might do best on their own.

Projects make it possible to offer a wide verity of subjects, determined by the interest of the students. It becomes the students' responsibility to develop the project with available resources, not the instructor.

With a wide verity of learning environments, a student has greater opportunity to find a project that is in harmony with his natural talent. All teenagers want to learn, be creative and productive, but they need opportunity.

Benefits of project base education:

- *Project base education is empowering students to learn, where the instructor is a coach, a facilitator.*

- *Projects make it possible to discover one's natural talent and personal interest.*

- *Projects make it possible to discover one's learning personality.*

- *Projects have a goal that is based on man's desire to be a winner. Self-satisfaction is a powerful motivator.*

- *Projects are learning tools that is motivated by curiosity.*

- *Projects work with the forces of nature and nature is the instructor.*

- *Projects give students opportunity to learn with objects. Not everyone is a literary intellectual.*

- *Successful projects are the results of failure and learning to bounce back from it.*

- *Projects require a plan, which includes ways to acquire needed knowledge and skills.*

- *Projects have all the motor skills that it takes to start and run a business or become a valuable employee, skilled or unskilled.*

Society must ABANDON the belief that:

- students must meet a predetermined level of academic standards by a selected age. (everyone is different)

- students who don't meet those standards are failures. (they aren't)

- all students can learn in a passive environment. (they can't)

- a diploma is more valuable than positive self-esteem. (it isn't) In the blue-collar world, employers base hiring on attitudes, not class grades or diplomas.

- all students can relate classroom studies to real world experiences. (they can't)

- standardized test measures knowledge and/or potential success level. (it doesn't)

- number of years spent in classrooms and class grade level determines success level in the real world. (it doesn't)

- academics must be mastered before other opportunity is offered. (some people learn by doing)

- teenagers are not mature enough to make decisions that determine their destiny. (give them a chance)

Teenagers Embrace Self-fulfilling Prophecy

Academic based education is designed to remove barriers and promote a productive lifestyle. This is true for a majority of students. For others, academic priority builds barriers that are almost impossible to overcome. Self-fulfilling prophecy has a powerful influence on youth and when they are told they are failures most of their young lives, they believe it and act accordingly. Project based education can give some a second chance.

Learning with Responsibility

Learning with responsibility is the future. Our society is becoming too complex for authority control to be efficient. Leadership cannot comprehend, let alone implement, the wide variety of alternatives available. People with hands-on involvement are the best one's to explore ways to be efficient, but the system has to be organized to allow affected people to take responsibility. This includes students and workplace employees.

There have been many attempts by organizations to implement worker responsibility programs, only to see them fail. They failed because leadership will not give up control and delegate responsibility. Visit Workplace Motivation

Today, the education system must adapt to the same kind of learning environment that business are adapting to, team responsibility. Teenagers that experience responsibility in high school will be the super efficient leaders of the 21st century. This concept recognizes the fact that there is more to education than academics. More Information

The right project can motivate anyone to excel. The curriculum assumed students would not finish high school. For this reason, farm management and engineering skills were taught in grade school. Today's young people have to attend college for specialized learning opportunity.

Project-Based Education: An Alternative to Academic-Based Education. Classroom environments require students to take an interest in instructors programs. In high school, there is little opportunity for students' interest to be recognized or be developed. As a result, students whose interests are out of harmony with the classroom take no interest in what instructors are trying to do. **CONFLICT!** Students then **GIVE UP**, are labeled failures, and are considered social outcasts. **Project-Based Education can offer alternatives that redirect rebellious attitudes into productive skills.** http://www.motivation-tools.com/youth/learning_personality.htm

Our Learning Personality. http://www.motivation-tools.com/youth/learning_tools.htm **Explanation of term:** Every individual has not only a physical personality that is different from everyone else; we also have a **learning personality** that is different from everyone else. Our learning personality is the combination of natural talent, social environment, character, personal interest, motivation, current opportunity, and how the brain processes information. Everyone could find a productive lifestyle if they could find a learning process with opportunities that match their learning personality. Also includes a chart on **"Perceived** People who love to learn do not depend on classrooms for knowledge; they develop a learning style that is in harmony with their learning personality. They develop learning tools that works for them. Learning by doing leads to above average opportunity and wages.

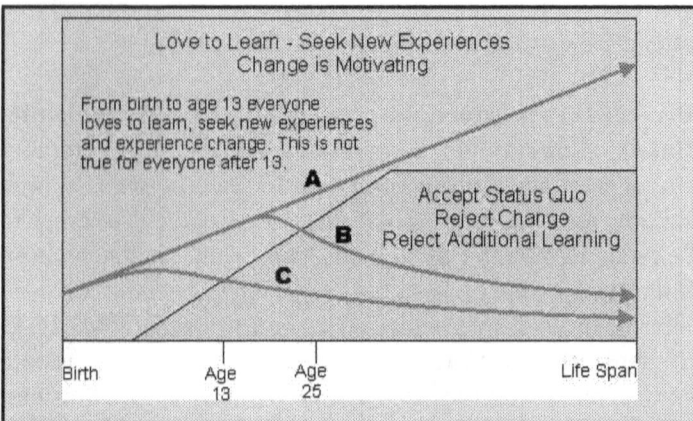

Love to Learn - Seek New Experiences
Change is Motivating

From birth to age 13 everyone loves to learn, seek new experiences and experience change. This is not true for everyone after 13.

A

Accept Status Quo
Reject Change
Reject Additional Learning

B

C

Birth   Age 13   Age 25   Life Span

A - Desire to learn is maintained over a lifetime. This person's education is not based on years spent in classrooms; it is based on a persistent desire to maintain a continuous natural learning environment. The result is above average wages. These are the CEO's, and other achievers who have a vision and know how to get things done. These people are independent thinkers and doers. They are NOT dependent on others for knowledge or opportunity, they do not wait for opportunity to come their way, they go after it.

B - Desire to learn is maintained until a professional skill is mastered that meets basic needs, then it dies. This person is the typical professional that makes average wages.

C - Desire to learn dies before a professional skill is mastered. This person makes below average wages.

These two groups are dependent on others for opportunity. They can rise no higher than the image they have of themselves, which is based on other's opinions. Associates tell them their limits, which they believe and accept. They do not make efficient use of natural learning tools because they were taught to depend on others for knowledge. As a result, they focus on protecting their **comfort zone** and the status quo.

The difference between group **"A"** and **"B, C"** is a <u>vision</u> that motivates. People who have a vision control their destiny and lifestyle. For people without a vision, their destiny and **lifestyle** is controlled by others.

Today, our education system is preoccupied with standardized tests. The goal is to bring failing students from group **"C"** up to **"B,"** which is minimum academic standards. These tests are producing a mind-set in all students to accept the status quo. As a result, students that would be in group **"A"** are dragged down to **"B."** They drop any visionary ideas they may have had and focus on testing. The goal should be to give students the tools to move from **"B, C"** to **"A."** This requires a different type of education.

Today's education goal is to get students to pass standardized test. The results influence teachers' bonuses and school funding. When the curriculum is controlled by funding, teaching students to have a vision is no longer feasible, because it **can't be measured**.

The below learning tools are highly effective in social environments that are in harmony with <u>learning personality</u>. They produce CEO's or criminals depending on their social environment.

Intelligence in Different Social Environments."

<u>Project-Based Education</u>. The program is based on what interests and motivates the student. Because the instructor cannot customize lesson plans for each student, he must implement student empowerment. It becomes the student's responsibility to develop and research projects and develop a plan of action. The instructor acts as a coach or facilitator. Instructors take an interest in students' projects instead of students having to take an interest in topics handed down by administrators. http://www.motivation-tools.com/youth/learning_tools.htm

Projects and the Self-Educated Man. When faced with a challenge, man has the power to learn without an instructor. This is how Abraham Lincoln, Thomas Edison, Henry Ford, and thousands of other highly successful people became educated. http://www.motivation-tools.com/youth/project_challenge.html

Tools of People Who Love to Learn. People who love to learn do not depend on classrooms for knowledge; they develop a learning style that is in harmony with their learning personality. They develop learning tools that work for them. Skills that bring above-average wages are the result of learning by doing in natural learning environments. http://www.motivationtools.com/youth/project_challenge.html

Education first then opportunity? Or opportunity first then education?

Some people can learn without knowing the reason why; for them, education first then opportunity. Classrooms are examples of education first. Technical skills are acquired as needed.

Some people need to know why before anything sticks. For them, opportunity first followed by training. Apprentice programs are examples of opportunity first. Academics are acquired as needed.

Opportunity First versus Academics First. People whose ideas changed the way we live have always been in conflict with classroom environments. Innovators are not A-students; they do not accept the classroom formula for success. They learn with projects, which require opportunity first. http://www.motivationtools.com/youth/project_challenge.html

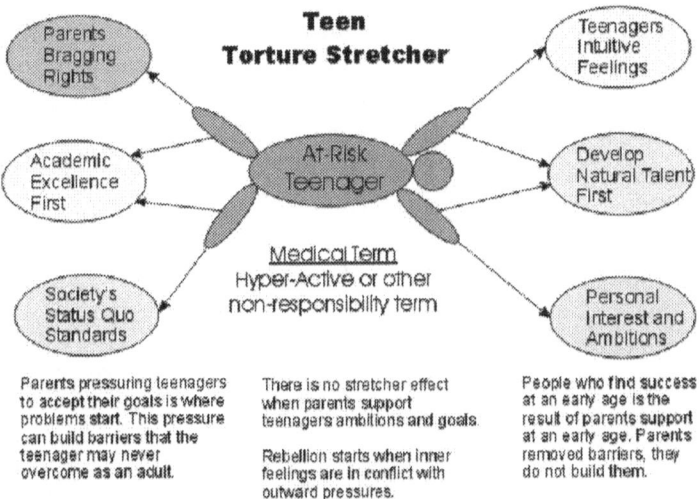

Teen Torture Stretcher

Parents Bragging Rights

Teenagers Intuitive Feelings

Academic Excellence First

At-Risk Teenager

Develop Natural Talent First

Society's Status Quo Standards

Medical Term
Hyper-Active or other non-responsibility term

Personal Interest and Ambitions

Parents pressuring teenagers to accept their goals is where problems start. This pressure can build barriers that the teenager may never overcome as an adult.

There is no stretcher effect when parents support teenagers ambitions and goals.

Rebellion starts when inner feelings are in conflict with outward pressures.

People who find success at an early age is the result of parents support at an early age. Parents removed barriers, they do not build them.

The At-Risk Student May Be a Genius. Today, pressure is on all students to stay in school no matter how strong the failure label becomes. Students being told they are a failure five times a day, five days a week, will develop low self-esteem that will do more harm than a diploma will do good. Self-fulfilling prophecies will seal their fate. Dropouts who become achievers will spend ten to fifteen years of persistent effort to overcome their negative self-esteem. Most adults can't escape negative self-esteem because they accepted the failure label that was placed on them as teenagers.

http://www.motivationtools.com/youth/project_challenge.html

Barriers to Motivation. Parents that Build Barriers Compared to Parents that Remove Barriers, this is a must read go to this link. http://www.motivation-tools.com/youth/youth_barriers.htm

At-Risk Students Who Find Success. **How & Why?**
There is a small percentage of at-risk teenagers who fall through the education system cracks, drop out, and succeed, some becoming self-made millionaires. To rise above the crowd requires the ability to acquire and process knowledge. Successful people who were labeled at risk by the education system use projects to develop valuable skills.

http://www.motivationtools.com/youth/project_challenge.html

A Dysfunctional Education System Produces Dysfunctional Teenagers

Society expects teenagers to adapt to a one-system-for-all no matter how dysfunctional the system may be. A flexible system can create opportunity for various <u>learning personalities</u>, thereby motivating them to excel. http://www.motivationtools.com/youth/project_challenge.html

The Case for Alternative Education. Because of smoke and mirrors by politically controlled education systems, the percentage of teenagers trying to be better students is shrinking. The percentages of students that give up are growing. Students not supporting classroom boredom are labeled failures, considered outcasts, and this self-fulfilling prophecy will prove everyone right. http://www.motivationtools.com/youth/project_challenge.html

Teaching Young Students to be Failures. Every teenager wants to be an achiever and be somebody. For many, the classroom environment labels them failures. No one likes to be labeled a failure, so these teenagers join street gangs, where they are considered heroes among their peers. They become achievers in criminal activity.

http://www.motivationtools.com/youth/project_challenge.
html

What is Education? What can be considered a quality education? A quality education is custom designed and addresses the unique abilities of each student. Custom education evaluates natural talent and how a student learns. This is why home-schooled students outperform classroom students. Parents learn what works and does not work, then focus on what works. With this method, students develop a love to learn, and learning becomes a lifelong process.

http://www.motivationtools.com/youth/project_challenge.
html

Education Goals Need to be Revised. From the beginning of man to the late 1800s, formal education institutions were the only source of information, and attending these institutions was the only way to acquire information. The students were, and are today, learners of facts. Times have changed.

http://www.motivationtools.com/youth/project_challenge.
html

Drugging Students to Accept the Status Quo. Society is now drugging our youth with behavior-control pills, nullifying the skill that makes them creative. They learn to accept the status quo. This new generation may make a comfortable living, but they will have lost the ability to be an innovator. Soon, America will have a generation of people who can earn A's in the classroom, but have no vision in the real world.

Intellectuals, for intellectuals, design classroom education. For intellectual teenagers, the education system inspires a vision, helps them discover their natural talent, gives them an opportunity to develop it, and then helps them find their first job, thereby helping them to fulfill their natural desire to excel. The system does NOT do the same for non-intellectuals.

Today, **30 percent** of teenagers will drop out of high school. They will never adapt to passive classroom environments, no matter what type of academic program are offered—they are NOT intellectuals! The alternative is to create an environment where non-intellectual teenagers can discover their natural talent. This can be done with project-based education, where academics are a by-product.

In today's education system, academics have priority and self-discovery is a by-product.

Society must ABANDON the belief that:
Students must meet a predetermined level of academic standards by a selected age. Students who don't meet those standards are failures—wrong.

A diploma is more valuable than positive self-esteem—wrong. In the blue-collar world, employers base hiring on attitudes, not class grades or diplomas. All students can learn in a passive environment (i.e., listening to lectures)—they can't. A standardized test measures knowledge and/or potential success level—it doesn't. A *number* of years spent in classrooms and class grade level determines success level in the real world—it doesn't. Academics must be mastered before other opportunity is offered. Many successful people found opportunity first, and then mastered academics later in life. Teenagers are not mature enough to make decisions that determine their destiny—many are. We must change our attitudes concerning learning and education to move forward as a country and a society.

The following people were self-educated, using projects as their education tool. Academic achievement was a by-product. Some never went to school, while others did not go beyond high school. The ideas of these people changed the way we live.

Frederick Douglass (1818-1895), born a slave
Abraham Lincoln
Thomas Edison
Alexander Graham Bell
Orville and Wilbur Wright
Henry Ford
Charles Lindbergh
Walt Disney
Chuck Yeager—the first man to fly faster than sound
Steve Jobs—inventor of the personal computer
Bill Gates—founder of Microsoft
Kirk Kerkorian—Hollywood billionaire investor
Harry Wayne Huizenga—Founder of Blockbuster Video

Before 1960, self-education was a highly desirable and acceptable form of education. When the astronauts were chosen, the first requirement was a college education. This eliminated the man who made space flight possible, Chuck Yeager. His formal education was limited to high school. From that time on, society no longer recognized self-educated people. Forty years later, it is becoming a lost art.

Fact: Self-made millionaires are not A-students in the classroom. The way they process knowledge is in conflict with classroom priorities. The self-made millionaire has a vision, then he researches specific knowledge, applies intuitive knowledge, and process all the elements, searching for a workable solution. Finding alternative ways to do common tasks makes millionaires. The secret is vision, research, and processing, not pre-stored knowledge.

The typical employer wants employees with dictionary knowledge, not visionaries. They want employees who follow orders, are willing to do repetitive tasks, be happy with a limited role, and accept the status quo. Repetitive tasks equal efficiency, and this is where profits are made. Also, the status quo prevents the exposure of blunders by leaders. Too many blunders and profits disappear. In a status quo environment, visionaries become bored quickly and soon receive the troublemaker label by offering alternatives or exposing blunders, sometimes leading to dismissal; yet their ideas increase efficiency and create new sources of profits for the company. In the long haul, visionaries are the ones who make above-average wages no matter what their formal education level. The education system now has the tools to kill off this type of person: behavior-control drugs! As these students move into the workforce, status quo and blunders will kill off the typical business.

What can be considered a quality education? A quality education is a custom design that addresses the unique abilities of each student and has a positive emotional experience. Custom education evaluates natural talent and how the student learns. This is why home-schooled students outperform classroom students. Parents learn what works and does not work, then focus on what works. With this method, students develop a love to learn, and learning becomes a lifelong process.

American students score below many other countries in math and science. What is not understood is that low-scoring students are technicians who continue to keep this nation a leader of technology. That's because the same students who show limited interest in learning academics demonstrate great skills and confidence in creating new concepts. Creating the *new* motivates technicians, whereas mastering the *old* doesn't.

Policies that created wealth during the industrial age are leading individuals, companies, and society into dead-end traps. The industrial age is gone and we are entering the technological age. Today, narrow profit margins and fast-changing technologies are forcing individuals and companies to replace the status quo with continuous change. Businesses must implement leadership styles that maintain the employee's love to learn and an environment where change motivates people, because continuous change means efficiency during the twenty-first century.

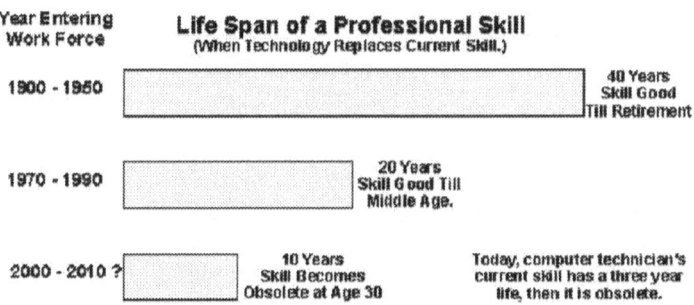

The present education system served us well when a professional skill was good till retirement. When a skill becomes obsolete in a few years, then other methods of learning are required. A person cannot keep going back to the classroom every time new technology replaces current skill. We are entering the age where we need continuous education. Continuous education requires the ability to learn without dependency on instructors, which is learning how to learn. Computer technicians must use self-education techniques to learn beyond the basics.

Drugging Students to Accept the Status Quo. Society is now drugging our youth with behavior-control pills, nullifying the skill that makes them creative. They learn to accept the status quo. This new generation may make a comfortable living, but they will have lost the ability to be an innovator. Soon, America will have a generation of people who can earn A's in the classroom, but have no vision in the real world. Drugs do not address underlying problems; they change current behavior by slowing brain activity, while letting the original problem simmer. Somewhere in life, this suppression will explode with destructive results. In the adult world, dependency on drugs kills ambitions. There is no free ride to success.

There is a fine line between legal drugs to control behavior and illegal drugs that make people feel good. The users of illegal drugs are content to live in a world of artificial highs. Today's society is teaching children to live in a world of artificial highs with legal drugs. They may get passing grades in school and land their first job. This may be the end of benefits and the beginning of destruction. In the real world, taking pills to solve problems does not solve anything; it delays them until they explode.

Now you have the whole story. Are you going to continue to do nothing and let this continue? You had better get involved now.

Get a couple of leader types have meetings or attend school board meetings. Demand change on a local level. Change begins with you—that's right, you. All change begins with the action of the first person. No more damn excuses. We need to save our children. I end this chapter with tears.

CHAPTER FOUR

LAW

Law. That's right: law. What is law, where did it come from, and why? First the definition of law according to *Webster's*: A rule of conduct or procedure established by custom, agreement, or authority. The body of rules and principles governing the affairs of a community and enforced by a political authority; a legal system: *international law*, the **condition of social order** and justice created by adherence to such a system.

Are you in tears yet? Bored? Just wait. Read on. You won't be, I assure you. You and I are getting screwed every day by some law. Who's the good guy? Who's the bad guy? Oh, and who cares anyway?

Law dates back to the very beginning of recorded history.

2,350 B.C.: Urukagina's Code

This code has never been discovered but it is mentioned in other documents as a consolidation of existing "ordinances" or laws laid down by Mesopotamian kings. An administrative reform document was discovered which showed that citizens were allowed to know why certain actions were punished. It was also harsh by modern standards. Thieves and adulteresses were to be stoned to death with stones inscribed with the name of their crime. The code confirmed that the "king was appointed by the gods."

2,050 B.C.: Ur-Nammu's Code

The earliest known written legal code, of which a copy has been found, albeit a copy in such poor shape that only five articles can be deciphered. Archaeological evidence shows that it was supported by an advanced legal system, which included specialized judges, the giving of testimony under oath, the proper form of judicial decisions, and the ability of the judges to order that damages be paid to a victim by the guilty party. The code allowed for the dismissal of corrupt men, protection for the poor, and a punishment system where the punishment is proportionate to the crime. Although it is called "Ur-Nammu's Code," historians generally agree that it was written by his son Shugli. Sounds like something we need now. The current system of Law in the USA only benefits those who are financially able to pay for legal representation.

1,850 B.C.: The Earliest Known Legal Decision

A clay tablet reveals the case, in 1,850 B.C., of the murder of a temple employee by three men. The victim's wife knew of the murder but remained silent. Eventually, the crime came to light and the men and woman were charged with murder. Nine witnesses testified against the men and woman and asked for the death penalty for all four. But the wife had two witnesses who told the court that she had been abused by her husband, that she was not part of the murder, and that she was even worse off after her husband's death. The men were executed in front of the victim's house, but the woman was spared. Now that's swift justice.

1,700 B.C.: Hammurabi's Code

This Babylonian king came to power in 1,750 B.C. Under his rule, a code of laws was developed and carved on a huge rock column. The expression "an eye for an eye" has come to symbolize the principle behind Hammurabi's code. It contains 282 clauses regulating a vast array of obligations, professions, and rights including commerce, slavery, marriage, theft, and debts. The punishments are, by modern standards, barbaric. The punishment for theft was the cutting off of a finger or a hand. A man's lower lip was cut off if he kissed a married woman. Cutting out the tongue punished defamation. If a house collapsed because the builder did not make it strong enough, killing the owner, the builder was put to death. If the owner's son died, then the builder's son was executed. **You're not bored now, are you?**

1,300 B.C.: The Ten Commandments

According to the Bible, it was in approximately 1,300 B.C. that Moses received a list of ten laws directly from God. These laws were known as the Ten Commandments and were transcribed as part of the books of Moses, which later became part of the Bible. Many of the Ten Commandments continue in the form of modern laws such as "thou shalt not kill" (modern society severely punishes the crime of murder), "thou shalt not commit adultery" (modern society allows a divorce on this grounds), and "thou shalt not steal" (modern society punishes theft as a crime). The Bible chapter that contains the Ten Commandments (Exodus) follows the recitation of the commandments with a complete set of legal rules, which are based on the "eye for an eye, tooth for a tooth" legal philosophy of Hammurabi's Code.

1,280 B.C. to 880 B.C.: The Laws of Manu

It has not yet been possible to pinpoint exactly when India's great laws of Manu were written. The laws were a written compilation of known legal rules that had been passed on from generation to generation. They formed the basis of the caste system in India, where people were classified by their social standing, and regulated almost all facets of India's society from contracts to criminal law. The laws of Manu used punishment sparingly, and only as a last resort and rarely sadistically. Amputation, though, was a possible sentence. The members of the higher castes were punished more severely than those of the lower castes.

621 B.C.: Draco's Law

This Greek citizen was chosen to write a code of law for Athens (Greece). The penalty for many offences was death; so severe, that the word "draconian" comes from his name and has come to mean, in the English language, an unreasonably harsh law. His laws were the first written laws of Greece. These laws introduced the state's exclusive role in punishing persons accused of crime instead of relying on private justice. The citizens adored Draco and upon entering an auditorium one day to attend a reception in his honour, the citizens of Athens showered him with their hats and cloaks as was their customary way to show appreciation. By the time they dug him out from under the clothing, he had been smothered to death.

Where is this going? Hang on—you will see in a minute.

600 B.C.: Lycergus' Law

This king of Sparta (southern Greece) was a renowned lawgiver. His laws were never written, just transmitted orally, and were designed to support the military vocation of Sparta. It held that women had a duty to have children, and that children born with deformities were killed. Children became wards of Sparta at the age of seven to prepare them for military duty. The greatest crime of all was retreat in battle. The Laws of Lycergus controlled virtually every aspect of the lives of citizens of Sparta.

550 B.C.: Solon's Laws

Solon was an Athenian statesman and lawmaker. He further refined Draco's laws and is credited with "democratizing" justice by making the courts more accessible to citizens.

536 B.C.: The Book of Punishments

A legal book printed in China that limited the ways to punish someone when they had been convicted of a serious crime. They included tattooing, cutting off of the nose, castration, feet amputation, and death.

450 B.C.: The Twelve Tables

Ten Roman men were given wide powers to write the laws that were to govern Romans. They came up with ten laws, to which two were later added. **These laws are considered the foundation of all modern public and private law.** They promoted the organization of public prosecution of crimes, and instituted a system whereby injured parties could seek compensation from their aggressors. More importantly, they protected the lower class (plebes) from the legal abuses of the ruling class (the patricians) especially in the enforcement of debts. From that point on, **a basic principle of Roman law is that the law must be written and justice cannot be left in the hands of judges alone to interpret.** It also prohibited interclass marriages, seriously punished theft, and gave fathers the right of life or death over his sons. The Twelve Tables also punished the misuse of magic! Written on wood and bronze tablets, the Twelve Tables survived almost 1,000 years until destroyed by invading Gauls in 390.

A.D. 529: Justinian's Code

This emperor of Byzantium is best remembered for his codification of Roman law in a series of books called *Corpus Juris Civilis*. His collection served as an important basis for law in contemporary society, and was inspired by **logic-based, Greek legal principles.** Many legal maxims still in use today are derived from Justinian's Code. His work inspired the modern concept and, indeed, the very spelling of "justice." This Roman code survived in many parts of Germany until 1900, and important traces of it can be found in the law of Italy, Scotland, South Africa, and Quebec. Roman law formed the base of civil law, one of the two main legal systems to govern modern society in Western civilization (the other being English common law). A quote: "The things which are common to all (and not capable of being owned) are: the air, running water, the sea, and the seashores."

A.D. 1100: First Law School

In medieval Italy, students of law would hire a teacher to teach them Roman law, especially Justinian's Code, *Corpus Juris Civilis*. One teacher, known as Irnerius, was particularly popular, and students began to flock to him from all over Europe. He taught in Bologna, and the surge of students meant that he had to hire other teachers to form the world's first law school. By 1150, his law school had over 10,000 students and contributed to the revival of the *Corpus Juris Civilis* and the spread of Roman law throughout Europe!

A.D. 1215: Magna Carta

At Runneymede, England, on June 15, 1215, King John of England signed the Magna Carta, in which he conceded a number of legal rights to his barons and to the people. In order to finance his foreign wars, King John had taxed abusively. His barons threatened rebellion and coerced the king into committing to rudimentary judicial guarantees such as the freedom of the church, fair taxation, controls over imprisonment (habeas corpus), and the right to all merchants to come and go freely except in time of war. The Magna Carta had sixty-one clauses, the most important of which may have been number thirty-nine: "No freeman shall be captured or imprisoned ... except by lawful judgement of his peers or by the law of the land." It was the first time a king allowed that even he could be compelled to observe a law, or that the barons were allowed to "distrain and distress him in every possible way," just short of a legal right to rebellion. Once sworn to the document, letters were sent to all sheriffs ordering them to read the charter aloud in public. It has been called the "blueprint of English common law" and was even recently pleaded in an English case.

A.D. 1765: Blackstone's Commentaries on the Laws of England

This British barrister set about writing down the entire English law in a four-volume set, in easy-to-read English, thus making the law suddenly accessible to the common man. His research also made the book a must-read for lawyers and law students alike. It was re-published many times. Through it, English law was readily imported to the British colonies, and, in fact, it is said that Blackstone's *Commentaries* was the law in the American colonies for the first century of American independence. The *Commentaries* also allows us to witness the exact state of British law at that time on such things as the total legal submission of a wife to her husband, as was then considered natural law.

A.D. 1776: <u>The American Declaration of Independence</u>

"We the people," starts the Declaration of Independence proclaimed on July 4, 1776. The Declaration was a statement to the effect that "all political connection between (the United Colonies) and the State of Great Britain is and ought to be dissolved" and that a new state, the United States, had begun. It remains a remarkable legal document in that it is the first time a government has rebuked the medieval theory that certain people possessed by right the power to rule others. "All men are created equal," rings the Declaration, and have "unalienable rights, that among these are life, liberty, and the pursuit of happiness. That to secure these rights, governments are instituted among men, deriving their powers from the consent of the governed."

Read this at least once in your life. It may have a serious effect on you and your family.

The Declaration of Independence
of the Thirteen Colonies

Note: The following is the verbatim text of the Declaration of Independence, approved by the U.S. Congress on July 4, 1776. Some capitalization has been adjusted to make the document easier to read (in 1776, writers often capitalized words to add emphasis as we might use bold or italics). We've also introduced Thomas Jefferson's famous 220-year-old document to HTML language by using bullets where a list is implied in the body of the Declaration of Independence.

This text is often cited as a masterpiece of legal writing. Lloyd Duhaime, April 21, 2001.

The unanimous Declaration of the thirteen United States of America (New Hampshire, Massachusetts, Rhode Island, Connecticut, New York, New Jersey, Pennsylvania, Delaware, Maryland, Virginia, North Carolina, South Carolina, and Georgia).

When in the course of human events, it becomes necessary for one people to dissolve the political bands which have connected them with another, and to assume among the powers of the Earth, the separate and equal station to which the laws of nature and of nature's God entitle them, a decent respect to the opinions of mankind requires that they should declare the causes which impel them to the separation.

We hold these truths to be self-evident, that all men are created equal, that they are endowed by their Creator with certain unalienable rights, that among these are life, liberty, and the pursuit of happiness.

That to secure these rights, governments are instituted among men, deriving their just powers from the consent of the governed. That whenever any form of government becomes destructive of these ends, it is the right of the people to alter or to abolish it, and to institute new government, laying its foundation on such principles and organizing its powers in such form, as to them shall seem most likely to effect their safety and happiness.

Prudence, indeed, will dictate that governments long established should not be changed for light and transient causes; and accordingly all experience hath shewn, that mankind are more disposed to suffer, while evils are sufferable, than to right themselves by abolishing the forms to which they are accustomed.

But when a long train of abuses and usurpations, pursuing invariably the same object evinces a design to reduce them under absolute despotism, it is their right, it is their duty, to throw off such government, and to provide new Guards for their future security.

Such has been the patient sufferance of these colonies; and such is now the necessity that constrains them to alter their former systems of government. The history of the present king of Great Britain [George III] is a history of repeated injuries and usurpations, all having in direct object the establishment of an absolute tyranny over these states. To prove this, let facts be submitted to a candid world.

He has refused his assent to laws, the most wholesome and necessary for the public good.

He has forbidden his governors to pass laws of immediate and pressing importance, unless suspended in their operation till his assent should be obtained, and when so suspended, he has utterly neglected to attend to them.

He has refused to pass other laws for the accommodation of large districts of people, unless those people would relinquish the right of representation in the legislature, a right inestimable to them and formidable to tyrants only.

He has called together legislative bodies at places unusual, uncomfortable, and distant from the depository of their public records, for the sole purpose of fatiguing them into compliance with his measures.

He has dissolved representative houses repeatedly, for opposing with manly firmness his invasions on the rights of the people.

He has refused for a long time, after such dissolutions, to cause others to be elected; whereby the legislative powers, incapable of annihilation, have returned to the people at large for their exercise; the State remaining in the meantime exposed to all the dangers of invasion from without, and convulsions within.

He has endeavoured to prevent the population of these States; for that purpose obstructing the laws for naturalization of foreigners; refusing to pass others to encourage their migrations hither, and raising the conditions of new appropriations of lands.

He has obstructed the administration of justice, by refusing his assent to laws for establishing judiciary powers.

He has made judges dependent on his will alone, for the tenure of their offices, and the amount and payment of their salaries.

He has erected a multitude of new offices, and sent hither swarms of Officers to harass our people, and eat out their substance.

He has kept among us, in times of peace, standing armies, without the consent of our legislatures.

He has affected to render the military independent of and superior to the civil power.

He has combined with others to subject us to a jurisdiction foreign to our constitution and unacknowledged by our laws; giving his assent to their acts of pretended legislation:

o   For protecting them by a mock trial from punishment for any murders which they should commit on the inhabitants of these States:

o   For cutting off our trade with all parts of the world:

o   For imposing taxes on us without our consent:

o   For depriving us in many cases of the benefits of trial by jury:

o   For transporting us beyond seas to be tried for pretended offences:

o   For abolishing the free system of English laws in a neighbouring province, establishing therein an arbitrary government, and enlarging its boundaries so as to render it at once an example and fit instrument for introducing the same absolute rule into these colonies:

o   For taking away our Charters, abolishing our most valuable laws, and altering fundamentally the forms of our governments:

o   For suspending our own Legislatures, and declaring themselves invested with power to legislate for us in all cases whatsoever.

He has abdicated government here by declaring us out of his protection and waging war against us.

He has plundered our seas, ravaged our coasts, burnt our towns, and destroyed the lives of our people.

He is at this time transporting large armies of foreign mercenaries to complete the works of death, desolation, and tyranny, already begun with circumstances of cruelty and perfidy scarcely paralleled in the most barbarous ages, and totally unworthy the head of a civilized nation.

He has constrained our fellow citizens taken captive on the high seas to bear arms against their country, to become the executioners of their friends and brethren, or to fall themselves by their hands.

He has excited domestic insurrections amongst us, and has endeavoured to bring on the inhabitants of our frontiers, the merciless Indian savages, whose known rule of warfare is an undistinguished destruction of all ages, sexes, and conditions.

In every stage of these oppressions, we have petitioned for redress in the most humble terms. Our repeated petitions have been answered only by repeated injury. A Prince, whose character is thus marked by every act that may define a tyrant, is unfit to be the ruler of a free people.

Nor have We been wanting in attentions to our British brethren.

We have warned them from time to time of attempts by their legislature to extend an unwarrantable jurisdiction over us.

We have reminded them of the circumstances of our emigration and settlement here.

We have appealed to their native justice and magnanimity, and we have conjured them by the ties of our common kindred to disavow these usurpations, which would inevitably interrupt our connections and correspondence.

They too have been deaf to the voice of justice and of consanguinity. We must, therefore, acquiesce in the necessity, which denounces our separation, and hold them, as we hold the rest of mankind, enemies in war, in peace friends.

We, therefore, the Representatives of the United States of America, in General Congress, assembled, appealing to the Supreme Judge of the world for the rectitude of our intentions, do, in the name, and by the authority of the good people of these colonies, solemnly publish and declare.

That these United Colonies are, and of right ought to be free and independent States; that they are absolved from all allegiance to the British Crown, and that all political connection between them and the State of Great Britain is and ought to be totally dissolved; and that as free and independent States, they have full power to levy war, conclude peace, contract alliances, establish commerce, and to do all other acts and things which independent states may of right do.

And for the support of this Declaration, with a firm reliance on the protection of Divine Providence, we mutually pledge to each other our lives, our fortunes, and our sacred honor.

{Signed by representatives of New Hampshire, Massachusetts, Rhode Island, Connecticut, New York, New Jersey, Pennsylvania, Delaware, Maryland, Virginia, North Carolina, South Carolina, and Georgia.}

What a great beginning. Did you really get it? Did you really?

A.D. 1787: The Constitution of the United States of America

The seven articles of the American Constitution were signed in Philadelphia in 1787 and formed the basis of the first **republican government** in the world. The Constitution defined the institutions of government and the powers of each institution, carefully carving out the duties of the executive, legislative, and judicial branches. **The Constitution also declared that it was paramount to any other law, whether federal or state, and that it would override any other inconsistent law.** The American Constitution served as a model for the constitutions of many nations upon attaining independence or becoming democracies.

A.D. 1791: The American Bill of Rights

With the ink barely dry on the Constitution (signed only four years earlier), American statesmen amended their supreme law by declaring the rights of free speech, freedom of the press and of religion, a right to trial by one's peers (jury), and protection against "cruel and unusual punishment" or unreasonable searches or seizures. The ten amendments of the Bill of Rights became known as the first to ten amendment(s) respectively. The Bill of Rights influenced many modern charters or bills of rights around the world.

It appears that the most important aspect of law was to give the common man the full opportunity to plead the court even if he had very little or no financial means to pay for legal representation. This seems to be the most important theme.

What happened? Try going to court today without an attorney and see how long you last. The system has become so complicated that Mr. and Mrs. Joe America have no chance at all of self-representation before a court that was designed to protect them first. Millions of cases are lost for not appearing. Americans are now mostly afraid of the courts and feel there is no justice for them.

While criminals are provided free legal representation, the good guy gets screwed again. That's right. Who represents Mr. and Mrs. Joe America? No one, that's who. As we see, the earlier ideas of law and its dispensing were clearly set up to protect those less able to afford protection under the law and not just the criminals or lawbreakers. It was mostly set up to protect the good people of a society. We also have seen the complete injustice in the punishment aspects of almost all law. For example, in some murder cases the guilty will receive twelve years in prison when the criminal that commits a crime and shoots someone may receive twenty-five years in prison under the three-strikes-you're-out punishment system. What has gone wrong?

For the most part, the number one breakdowns in the original idea of law are the judges. That's right, the judges look at the decisions being handed down by judges who interpret the law in whatever manner or meaning they choose. The law is to be enforced as is. Enforcement was not intended to be left to the interpretation of judges. The law in America is very clear and needs to be enforced not reinterpreted.

Now, you read this very carefully, Mr. and Mrs. Joe America. Stop. Stop right now. Get involved, at least in letter-writing. Your chasing the dollar allows no time until the day these problems hit you right in the head.

Wake up. It's late, real late. Make the judges enforce the law; these people are not the great interpreters they would like us to think they are. If they refuse to do the job they were elected or chosen to do then have them removed. They can be removed. You must take action against these rogue judges. Every day we here of a judge somewhere in this country acting just as he pleases and not enforcing the law. Demand they be removed.

CHAPTER FIVE

THE

END

The end. That's right, the end. Get it crystal clear now, not later. It is very late. We now have political parties who no longer are interested in the good of the common workingman, or the common good and direction of the greatest nation in the history of planet Earth. Disagreement can be very productive; now, however, disagreement is only for the purpose of self-interest and the self-gain of a few at the expense of the nation's population.

Let's take a close look at the items that bring the end.

Tolerance. You think tolerance is going to solve problems when the rest of world is not tolerant? You had better wake up and smell the blood. Americans have become tolerant of everything as long as it doesn't directly affect them. Well, it does directly affect you.

1. Amnesty, driver's licenses, tax IDs, social security, equal treatment for **illegal aliens.** What nut job thinks this could ever be the right direction for any nation? Remember this: there has never been a nation in the history of the planet

that has survived trying to use multiple primary languages. None, ever—get it straight. The military should be assigned the responsibility of guarding the border, period. If someone is here illegally, go straight to jail and out of the country, and if they don't like where they're from let them change their country. Our forefathers put their lives on the line many times for our freedom and the building of this great nation. Get mad—damn mad and take action now.

2. Taxation has never helped a people in any way. Tax this tax that. Let's not forget one of the very main reasons our country came into being in the first place. Last time I checked it had lot to do with taxes. Companies leave states and countries because of taxation. People leave states and countries for the same reasons. Demand a low flat tax—an easy system limiting any deductions. You want to see more jobs and higher pay? Lower taxes. You—yes, you—are the most overtaxed person in the world currently. When are you going to put a stop to it? The politicians want your money— all of it, if they can get it. It's up to you stop buying this bull. Take action now, today. Don't go to sleep with out some action. I'm talking to you.

3. Education. **Lost** compared to other industrialized nations for math and science. No more. Demand the basics: reading, writing, and arithmetic. That's what put our nation number one in the world. Skip the new programs. They have proven beyond any doubt they don't work, they haven't worked, and they won't work. Give our children the tools for reading comprehension and the world is there creative playground; if you can comprehend what you read, the world is yours. Get the children who are not on grade level out of the classroom into a classroom where they can learn. We are a nation of achievers. Don't hold these children back because of some stupid rule-keeping children who are not on grade

level in the same classroom. Protect the teachers and our children now, right now. Now the political parties want there favorite "do boy" judges appointed. We need judges who will enforce the current law. The only test for any candidate for judgeship should be is his ability to read and enforce the current law. "Do boy" judges are not good for you or our country. The real test should be, could the candidate read and comprehend the law set before him? Remember judges can and should be swiftly removed from their office for violating current law. **No judges making laws of their own**. Remove them. If necessary, have them prosecuted.

I OFFER YOU AN INVITATION TO ACTION.

You now must take the responsibility of making our nation great again. You can only do this by your participation. Should you continue the apathetic attitudes you have demonstrated in the past, you will pay, your families will pay, and their families will pay?

PLEASE ACT NOW

THANK YOU

About the Author

Michael Lameyer is a direct to the point writer without deception. Michael Lameyer a Decorated Combat Veteran, Commercial Pilot, Flight Instructor, understands the importance of clear communications with clear concise instruction and the importance of taking positive action. Michael Lameyer is also a Certified Team USA Coach and has written many sports articles. Michael Lameyer has traveled Europe and the Pacific Rim Countries and has a very clear understanding of the what it will honestly take to maintain our leadership in a world developing at a very fast pace. Michael Lameyer married with four children understands the strength that family members can bring to each other and the many struggles that families face today.

Michael Lameyer offers real insight and solid workable solutions for many of the problems we face today as a people and a nation.